Minecraft:

Ultimate

Book of

Secrets

Marvelous Secrets
You Never Knew
About Befo

Minecraft
Library

Table of Contents

Introduction

Minecraft is full of secrets and Easter eggs. There are also many helpful tips that can be found! This guide will teach you about everything you didn't know about Minecraft!

Upside-down Mobs!

In creative mode, you can rename any Spawn Egg using an Anvil. Naming an egg "Grumm" will make the mob spawn upside-down!

Highway to Hell

To visit the Nether, Minecraft's version of Hell, Create a 4x5 Obsidian frame. Using Flint and Steel, light the inside of the frame to activate a Nether Portal!

Mob Mentality!

Injuring a Zombie-Pigman will make any nearby pigmen attack you!

Evil Step-Sisters

Witches will fight each other if you are in creative mode!

Creeper in the Sky with Diamonds

Creating a firework using a mob head will make the explosion look like a creeper!

Too Many Fireworks!

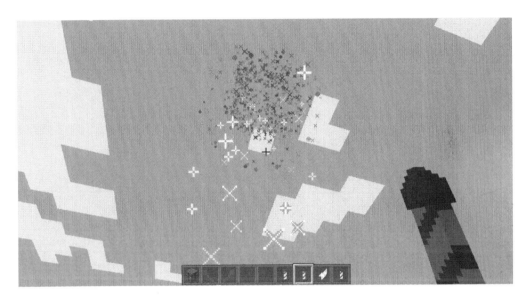

There are literally billions of different firework combinations that can be made. Fireworks can have different colors, shapes, durations, sizes and "twinkles"

Free Water?!

Infinite water sources can be created by digging a 2x2 hole, and putting water in 2 opposite corners. You can now draw as much water from it as you like!

Summon the Demon!

You can create the evil WIther mini-boss by placing 4 soul sand blocks in the formation below, then placing 3 Wither Skulls on top. This mini-boss is hard to defeat!

It's Christmas Already?!

Snowmen can be created by making a 1x2 structure with snow blocks then placing a pumpkin on top of that

The Iron Golem

Iron Golems Can be created by placing 4 Iron blocks in the formation below, then placing a pumpkin on top of the middle one!

Saving Slabs

Zombies will not burn in sunlight if they are standing on a slab block

Fuel Sources

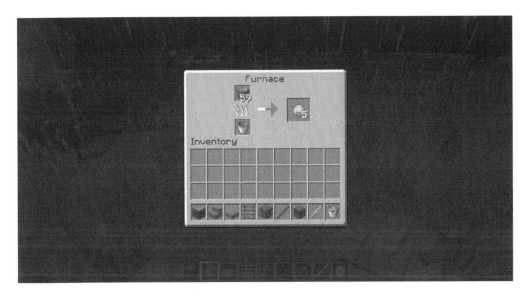

Almost any item made out of wood can be used in furnaces, except boats, signs and tools! Lava Buckets and Blaze Rods can also be used to smelt down your goods!

Sneaky Redstone

Redstone currents will travel through slabs, but not through blocks!

Need a light?

Even when not activated, beacons give off a greater light source than torches!

Here horsey horsey....

Don't have a saddle? Horses can still be tamed without needing a saddle! Just hop on the horse by right clicking. Keep doing this until the horse gives off heart icons. This means it has been tamed! You will still need a saddle to control the horse.

The Ender Portal

There is a mysterious place that can be visited in Minecraft called The End. To go there, one must either find an Ender Portal in a Stronghold, or create on if they are in creative mode. To create an Ender Portal, dig a 3x3 hole, then place Ender portal frames around the edges. Put an Eye of Ender in each frame, then the portal will activate!

The End

The End is a floating Island made out of Endstone. It is very small, and home to the Ender Dragon! The End is surrounded by The Void.

Don't Look Down!

Mobs will not jump off a tower more than 7 blocks high!

From a Distance

Wooden pressure plates can be activated by arrows

Trapping Chests

Unlike most blocks, chests can still be opened if there is a stair, leave, slab, fence or glowstone block above it.

No life vest needed

Mobs float in water. If they walk into water, they will always float to the top. Slimes are the only exception!

They grow ups so fast!

Use bonemeal on newly planted saplings to make the tree grow super fast!

Demolishing Cactus

A cactus will fall apart if a block is placed beside the base!

Quick Cutting Grass

Sick of all that grass? Use a water bucket to dump some water over them to cut them all down!

More Common than Iron!

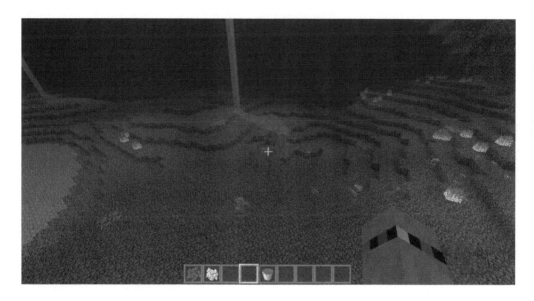

Quartz is the most common ore, but it can only be found in the Nether!

Battle Axe

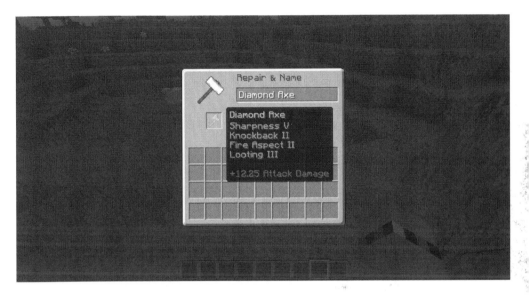

Using an Anvil and Enchanted Books,
weapon enchantments can be put on an axe!

One Book for All

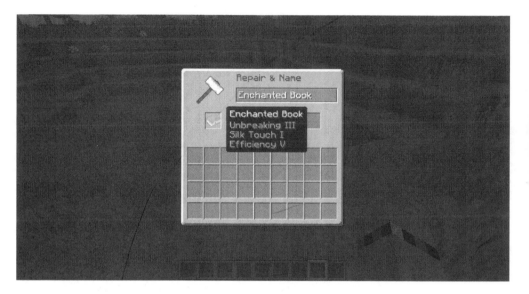

Do you have enchanted books taking up space in your inventory? Combine books together using an anvil to free up space!

Fire Retardant Baby

Baby Zombies have a 5% chance of
spawning, and they will not burn in the sunlight!

Heavy Duty Mobs

Skeletons and Zombies have a 17% chance of spawning with armour! Zombies also have a 5% chance of spawning with a weapon

Magical Scissors

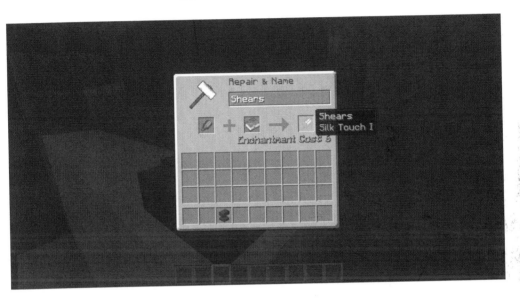

Shears can be enchanted with Silk Touch.
Enchanted Sears can be used to gather
flowers, leaves and ferns!

One-Touch Battery

Activated redstone lamps will activate other lamps that they are touching

Hidden Passages

Paintings can be used to conceal passageways! You can walk through paintings.

Don't be Such as Scaredy Cat!

Creepers are afraid of ocelots! If an ocelot is nearby, creepers will run away!

Lucky Level

Diamonds are most likely found on level 12!
To find your level, hit F3 and look for Y:

Ricochet TNT

Shooting an arrow at an activated TNT block will cause the arrow to ricochet!

Mob Protected Rails

Put slabs above your railway to prevent mobs from standing on the rails! You will not be hurt by the slabs

Night Light

A daylight sensor was added to Minecraft, which allows you to create an automatic night light!

Crazy Colored Sheep!

Sheep can naturally spawn pink, along with brown, white and black.

Hey, Open the Door!

Unlike Wooden Doors, Iron Doors can only be opened with pressure plates, buttons or levers.

No Gate? No Problem!

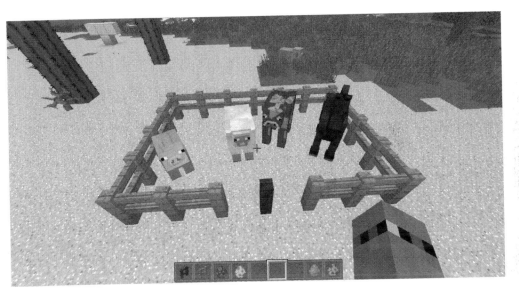

Create a nice fenced area for your animals without a gate, by using Nether Brick Fence! You can move in and out, but animals can't!

Can't Swim?

When crossing a body of water, you will move really slowly. Speed up the process by holding a bucket and right clicking!

Super Safe Garbage Can

Have a lot of trash in your inventory? Throw it at a cactus!

One way in, no way out!

Create a simple one-way door like this!

Quick Empty

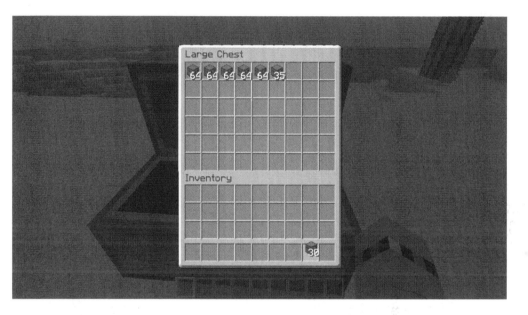

Have an inventory full of the same item? To quickly sort and empty them into a chest, pick one up, hold shift, then double click other stack!

Redstone Clock

To make a small redstone clock, make a 4x4 square by putting a block in each corner, then placing redstone repeaters in between, in a line. Activate it by using a torch, then put any redstone device you want on top!

Cased Water

If swimming down, you will move faster if the water is cased, but if swimming up, the case will slow you down!

Swimming Pool, Anyone?

To evenly fill up a large area with water, place the water on the diagonal (Shown by the diamond blocks)

Super Potions

Splash Potions have the greatest effect if launched out of a dispenser!

Cooked Vermin

The best way to kill Silverfish is with fire! Grab your flint and steel if you ever face a hoard of these beasts!

No More Cobwebs!

Use Shears to quickly get rid of all those pesky cobwebs!

Looking Horror in the Face

Wearing a pumpkin on your head will allow you to look right at an Enderman without him going nuts on you.

Sweeter Than Music

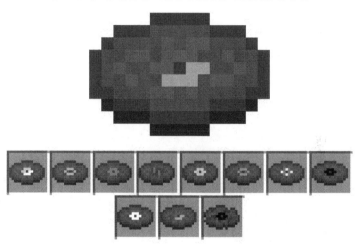

One may think: How can I get a skeleton to kill a creeper when they're both hostile towards me? Well it's hard, and the reward for this is a music disc.

Super Creep

Another crazy happenstance effect is the supercharged creeper. When they get hit by lightning, they become 10 times stronger and their explosion is HUGE!

Sneaky Builder

While building, hold the sneak button to not fall off the ledge. This is extremely helpful when building upward and not looking where you step.

Steve Comes with a GPS

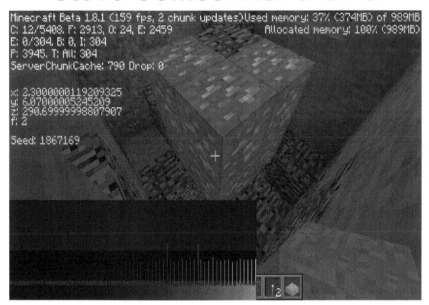

Hitting F3 gives you coordinates as well as many other details including the type of biome you're in.

Steve's Crazy One-way Mirror?

Creepers and Skeletons can't see you through glass. Like it's magically imbued glass or an overlooked feature. Probably the latter.

I Wouldn't Eat That If I Were You

Spider eyes fill you up around 90% but they also hurt you. Rotten flesh has a similar effect as well.

Scarecraft

On Halloween, there is a chance of any mob having pumpkins (lit and unlit) on their heads. Okay, it's not that scary, but those Endermen though...

Christmas At Mojang

On Christmas, chests will resemble presents.

Hot to the Touch

Tiny magma cubes, unlike tiny slime cubes, can still hurt you. Don't touch: Hot!

The Fabled Spider Jockey

You know the little guys that ride horses? Well imagine an undead one except his horse is a spider. That's a spider jockey. All skeletons have a 1% chance of spawning as a spider jockey.

Reminds Me of Home

Obsidian actually attracts mobs.

An Entire Island of Mushrooms You Say?

As rare as it is, it's actually real. These islands are full of tree sized mushrooms, Mycelium and weird cows called Mooshrooms that yield mushrooms instead of milk. It's a strange world.

You'd Think This Would Be More Sought After

The Mushroom Biomes actually spawn no hostile mobs on their own, which makes it even more of an oasis.

Mushrooms Like Dead Things

So rub some bone meal on a mushroom to make it the size of a tree.

Rainy Fishing Trip

Fishing in the rain yields much more fish.
Maybe they want to come up for a fresh drink.

Air Bucket

When swimming underwater and running out of air, just swipe your empty bucket and an air pocket will open for a split second which refills your air meter. Because who needs science?

Ship Wrecked No More

Line the edges of your docks with wool or soul sand and it won't break your boat if you hit them.

Frankenpig

It's alive! Well, it already was… If lightning hits a pig, he turns into a zombie pigman, which is also the only way to get one outside of the nether without spawning.

Why Don't You Just Get A Horse?

Saddles can be put on pigs. Before horses, saddles were just a rare item to show off. You couldn't even control where the pig went!

Enderfishing

Throwing your fishing line at an Enderman causes it to stay neutral. This is a good way to avoid having to fight one that's nearby.

Steve the Teleporter

If lava is a block between you and your minecart, just right click where the cart is and you will teleport straight through the lava without getting hurt.

Have You Played That Game Minceraft?

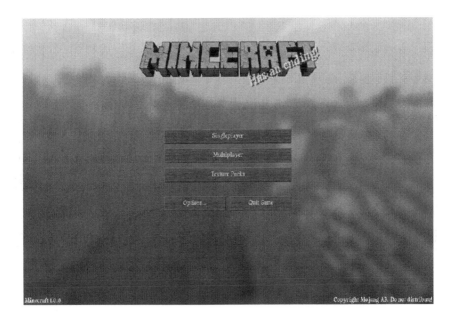

There is a 1 in 10,000 chance that the title will be misspelled in the opening screen.

Science In Motion

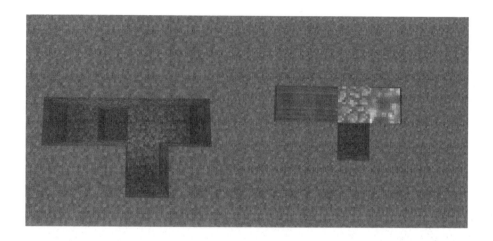

Lava + Water = Cobblestone. Just pour it on! No crafting needed.

Blocking in a Block World

Block with right click. It halves damage in case you can't get away in time.

Obsidian Creation

To make obsidian, just put water on source lava.

Charcoal

Smelting wood logs straight from the tree renders charcoal, an alternative to coal that works the same way.

They'll Need a Bigger Bomb

Obsidian structures are immune to creeper explosions.

Hacking Away

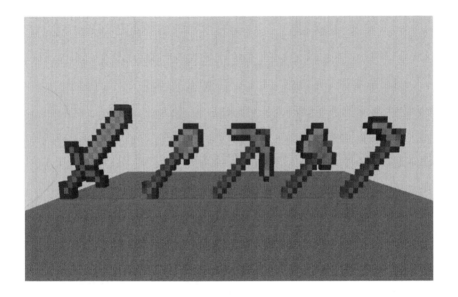

Every block has a tool that breaks it fastest. For stone, it's a pick. For dirt and sand it's a shovel. For cobwebs it's a sword.

Quit Your Squirming!

Jumping eats away at your hunger bar quicker. Sprinting does the same.

A Bit on Spawning

When on the hunt for food, leave one surviving animal of a kind. They will respawn much quicker than if you were to kill them all.

Logging

Leaving the lowest log block allows you to reach all segments of the tree trunk of a standard tree.

Minecraft Safety 101

Hostile mobs spawn in darkness. Keep
areas that you want safe marked with torches.

Hardcore

Golems, both iron and snow, are immune to fall damage. Remember this when kiting enemies.

You're Doing It Wrong

Don't whack a rock with a shovel. It'll break twice as fast

Horsing Around

Horses can wear armor and Donkeys can wear chests for carrying things.

Animals and Their Cravings

All animals are lured by different foods. Pigs by carrots, Cows by wheat, sheep by wheat and chicken

Conclusion

This book has provided you with some of the little-known secrets in Minecraft. Use these tips and trick to your advantage! Knowing these valuable pieces of information can make you an expert Minecrafter!

Bonus Section

If you liked this **Minecraft: Ultimate Book of Secrets**, check out other Amazing Minecraft Books from **Minecraft Library** © Creative Creators Community:

1. Minecraft: Ultimate Building Book

2. Minecraft: Ultimate Redstone Book

3. Minecraft: Ultimate Building Ideas

We're delighted to bring you the best knowledge and Minecraft experience. Enjoy!

Made in the USA
Lexington, KY
11 December 2014